√ dup

D1314942

When Mothers Touch Heaven

Joy Haney

New Leaf Press

When Mothers Touch Heaven

Printed in the United States of America

Cover Photography by Brodie Jayne's Photography Lodi, California.

Interior Photography, pages 8, 22, 32, 46, 64, 78, 86, 96, Jim Erickson/Corbis Stock Market; 14, 26, Jeanne Tiner; 54, 56, 63, Brodie Jayne's Photography

Cover Design by Farewell Communications

Interior Design by Bryan Miller

For more information write:
New Leaf Press
P.O. Box 726
Green Forest, Ark. 72638

Please visit our web site for
other great titles:
www.newleafpress.net

ISBN:
0-89221-495-3

Library of Congress:
00-102656

New Leaf Press

Contents

Preface

The most precious commodities that I have in this world are my wife, children, and the prayers of my mother. For you see, the secret to my so-called success is a mother's prayers. The Scripture tells us, "The effectual fervent prayer of a righteous man availeth much." I cannot think of any more righteous act than the prayers of a mother on behalf of her children.

There was a time in my life when I was just "going through the motions" and not really seeking God's will. I was just making some common sense decisions about what I wanted to do after I had had surgery on my back and could no longer raise cattle. My father had started a publishing company when I was in high school and I worked part-time in the warehouse, but I never really felt that I wanted to follow in my father's footsteps in a leadership position.

I was trying to decide what I wanted to do and actually had several good job offers from which to choose. I really don't remember a lot of details about how it happened or why, but over a period of six months or so my father signed the presidency of the company over to me. Something unexplainable happened inside my heart and I found myself working night and day — and really enjoying the challenges of publishing.

Two years later, my mother and I were sitting in my car discussing the future while planning my father's funeral. I said to her, "Wow! It sure is a good thing that I took over the company two years ago or it would be sitting in a tough position with no leadership." It was then that my mother revealed to me her prayers that she had been praying for my family, my sisters, and me. I was surprised because I didn't even know she had been praying for me. She told me that she had just prayed a very simple prayer to the Lord: "Reveal yourself to my son," for the Lord had spoken to her and now He needed to speak to me. It was then that this burden for Christian publishing was passed on from one generation to the next. Nine years have now gone by and I am thankful every day for the silent prayers of my mother to move God's will on my heart.

—Tim Dudley, Publisher

Introduction

It is not easy and never has been easy to be a mother, that is, the right kind of mother. To think that God places the breath of eternity into a small bundle of flesh and then gives it to a woman! She is to help train, influence, and teach that little bundle so it might grow up to be the person that God intended it to become. This is an awesome responsibility, but with the responsibility comes joy.

To be a mother is a bittersweet mixture. She is the one who comes up against the first try of the stubborn will. She will face all the ingenuity of a child as he works hard to get his way. It is the mother who sees the sweetness and the stubbornness portrayed at the same time. She must make the decision to not let the sweet smile outwit her at the game of life.

It is more than a game; it is war over the soul: the soul of her child. The war involves more than just mother and child. There is the sin element in which evil tries to triumph, but then there is the greater force, the power of God. She is not alone in her efforts. There is also the influence of the father, the grandparents, close relatives, friends, teachers, schools, and churches among other things. As much as a mother tries to raise her child right, there may come times when she must pray prayers of faith against sickness, evil influence, sin, stubbornness, and others' wrong influence. This book is about mothers who prayed and touched heaven for their child. God heard and did a miracle for them.

my mother's prayers never let go

I was raised in a pastor's home all my life. It was rather like living in a storefront window. We could never hide from the eyes of the people or leaders in the church. Everything we did seemed to be on display. Although I had the best parents in the world, the pressures involved with being a pastor's child and always being watched by everyone began to build in me. I felt as if I was in a box many times.

Sometimes growing up in the limelight, you can tend to focus on the negative, even though there are so many positive points.

Not only was my dad the pastor of a very large congregation, but he was also president of a Bible college and superintendent of a school. When I was about nineteen, a young man came my way. He seemed attracted to me and I was attracted to him. He was very handsome, and knew how to say the right words. He wooed me with roses, candy, and gifts. I was hooked and falling deeply in love.

Unfortunately my parents did not share the same feelings. At first they were more easy on me, but when I quit choir (which was my world because I love to sing) and became more and more distant from the things of God, they became very worried. When someone you love starts going backward instead of forward, you should start worrying.

By the time my parents tried to intervene, my mind was made up as to what I was going to do, and nothing was going to get in my way. I have always had a stubborn streak in me, which God can now use in a good way because I have totally surrendered to Him and His will for my life.

Back when I was going through this rebellious stage, I had a mind of my own and I would get my own way, even if it meant hurting the ones closest to me. It all started with my decision not to listen 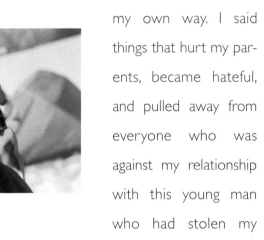 to my parents' counsel. My mother was the most vocal and talked to me over and over many times. We did not agree at all and this put a strain on our relationship. She even had a much-respected minister speak to me. My father finally counseled with me, but I became more and more stubborn, determined to go my own way. I said things that hurt my parents, became hateful, and pulled away from everyone who was against my relationship with this young man who had stolen my heart. During all of this, I remember I would cry and tell God that I wanted to do what was right, but I never yielded to His voice. There was a tug-of-war going on inside me. I was listening to music that fed my flesh and filled my mind with the things of this world, and this did not help either. I was becoming someone that I didn't even know.

It seemed that everyone had a word for me, and they would all say the same thing, which I resented. No one thought I should be pursuing a relationship with the man I loved. It was my love for him, my stubbornness, and the pressure that was mounting that caused me to do something drastic.

It was during the Christmas season and my parents had been invited to go to a Christmas musical in a city about 45 minutes from our home. No one was home and I quickly packed a suitcase and took off to another state hoping to escape the misery that I felt in my hometown.

My mother told me later that she had a premonition come over her and she told my father, "Something is happening. We have to go home." They could not leave because they had driven up with some friends. When they got home, it was too late to do anything.

Where I went I was welcomed with open arms by my boyfriend's parents. They showed me much kindness and treated me as a daughter. I soon secured a good job and met many different people. I went to a small church where the pastor and his wife were very kind to me. I really loved it there; it was so beautiful and peaceful, but there was still no peace in my heart. I learned how to smile even though my insides were falling apart, and was determined to stand strong in my decision because I never wanted to admit defeat.

I will never forget the night I received a call, and learned that my mother was at the airport waiting to be picked up by someone. I remember my heart dropped. I did not want anything to mess up my relationship.

Later in the evening my mother and I retired to my bedroom and climbed into bed. We talked through the night and I could see I was breaking her heart, but I still was not ready to give up my world with this young man. With tears running down her cheeks, she pled with me and held me in her arms. She prayed for me and did everything she could to take me back with her.

She left the next morning without me. There was snow everywhere. The roads were very icy, and there was also a part of me that felt icy, but another part felt very saddened. That was how far I had drifted from my mother. I was so hard against her and her words. I learned later that when she arrived back home without me, my sisters were very upset. They would write to me, telling me that my mother was praying and going on long fasts for me. I also remember receiving letters from so-called concerned people. All they did was preach to me and tell me how rebellious I was. This just pushed me farther away. I remember stating, "I'll never go back there. I hate them."

I remember I received a call from my father telling me that I was breaking my mother's heart and he asked me to come home. Despite the pleas from my family,

I remained unmoved and stubborn as a mule.

I found out later that my older sister had told my mom, "Just leave her alone. We have all tried to talk to her and she will not listen, besides she is killing you." But my mother just said, "I will never give up! My daughter will be back home. God will bring her back."

during the course of time, my relationship with my fiancé became strained and was not doing well at all. Because I did not want to accept defeat, I was willing to work on our relationship. My fiancé hardly went to church at all anymore, so I went to church without him. I had made many friends who were not Christians, so that did not help either.

Looking back over my life, I could not help think back to when I was eighteen years old. I was deeply involved with the youth group and the choir. It was normal to go to all-night prayer meetings and to fast several days. I was very dedicated. Nothing could turn me away from the things of God. I was sold out to God. I sang all the time for I loved to sing. I would dream about my future with God. I had many goals and wanted to go to college to further my education. Within a year, I had put my dreams aside, all for a great adventure that would just bring me to a dead-end of pain and sorrow. Of course, I did not see that at that time.

During this time, I remember after several months that my mother's letters were no longer preaching letters, just nice, chatty letters. There was no more advice, no scriptures, no admonition, just friendly news about home and people that I knew. (She later told me that God impressed her to not say another word about the problem to me, but only just to show me love.)

In the meantime, my fiance' and I were planning to be married. I wanted to be married in the fall. I remember my mother calling me and confronting me about getting married. It shocked me that she knew. She had found out somehow. Looking back, I have to ask myself, "What was I thinking? This woman, my mother, brings me into the world and then I don't even involve her with my marriage." Of course, it was hard since she did not agree with what I was doing.

by then I was living with an elderly woman who had a nice house. She also gave me her opinion about my relationship. I had not told her anything. She told me that she did not feel good about my relationship with my fiance'. She said she saw things that worried her. She also said I deserved someone better. Again, I became defensive and resented her. Here was a woman who knew nothing about my background, and she saw the same things that my family saw. Even though we did not get married that fall, we were still going together.

I remember one night sitting in my room. It was raining and I started reminiscing and started looking back over my life. I was not happy. I had held onto something that seemed so valuable to me that I was willing to give up everything for it. I remember looking out the window and just started crying like a baby.

Then I started sobbing. I felt as if I had come to the end. My relationship with my fiance' had become so sour. That big adventure had stripped me of everything and taken from me my dreams and my loved ones. I remember asking myself, "What are you doing with your life?" I had changed so much. I was not the girl that I used to be. I had become a person I did not even know. For the first time, I thought about going home and giving in to what I then called defeat, but I now know it was a step of courage.

I called home and told my parents that I was coming home. I remember my mother crying. She was so excited about my coming.

(I did not know at that time, but my mother had been on an extended fast for me and was praying non-stop.)

I did have mixed feelings while I was away from home, but I knew in my heart that I was doing the right thing. My fiance's parents even felt good about the move. They knew that spiritually I was in a dark tunnel going nowhere. I will never forget when my mother and all my sisters picked me up at the airport. I was so excited, but I was still cold on the outside. I had much pride. Therefore, I had to remain confident on the outside. My mother did not talk about anything from the past. We all just laughed and talked about things going on in my hometown.

That was the turning point for me of starting back to my dreams and to my precious family, and of course, turning slowly back to Jesus. My mother truly never gave up on me. I am sure she became weary of the fight, but she has always been a fighter. She had walked through the treacherous flames of hell to claim her lifeless daughter back. While Satan thought he had me there was my mother travailing for my soul. She would not let go until she saw me come back home and surrender my life to God.

Being home was not all easy, because not everyone was as loving as my mother and father were. There were those who tried to preach at me. Some had words of judgment, others had words of advice, but of course, there were so many who were very loving and glad to see me back.

One thing that I could never shut out of my ears were my mother's prayers. Growing up in our home with my siblings, many mornings we could hear her fervent prayers. They were not just the simple prayers she prays throughout the day, but she was fighting and warring in the spirit for her family. She has always been a woman of prayer. Even doing the dishes, she sometimes will begin to pray and talk to the Lord, not caring who is around.

Now I find myself praying every day like my mother prays. She taught me to pray with my whole heart and to shut out the world and enter into a place where only God is. It is a wonderful place. When the pressures come and I feel I cannot make it, I get on my knees and talk to my Heavenly Father. I know He will take complete control.

I truly believe that I am where I am today because of my mother's prayers. It was not just coincidence, but God heard the cries of a broken-hearted mother who refused to let go. So many people do not realize the power of prayer. I am a true testimony that prayer works!

When I was asked to write this testimony, I was reluctant at first, for this was a closed chapter that I did not want to re-open. But I know that my story will help others to see the power of prayer and to help their loved ones who have gone astray. It will also give honor to the most wonderful mother in the world who never gave up on her wavering daughter.

Thank you mother. I truly love you.

NAME WITHHELD

slashed, but not slain

On October 18, 1990, my secure world was interrupted by death and pierced with evil. I was not aware of the impending tragedy that would soon befall us, when I received a phone call from my sister who was caring for my mother who was very ill. She told me to come quickly, that Mother was near death. I had four wonderful days with my precious mother before she took her last breath.

After the funeral we flew home and agreed together that it was best to get back into schedule as soon as possible. The very next day after we went through the normal morning rituals, we made our way to our own Christian school where I was administrator. At 4:15 p.m. that day, my world fell apart even more.

One of the staff members came into my office and said, "Come quickly, something terrible has happened to Scott!" I flew out of my office to find my son, Jonathan Scott, sitting in the middle of the parking lot covered with blood! Suddenly I felt a weakness engulf me. "What has happened? What is going on?" I shouted.

In front of our church, a group of five gang members had beaten my son and slashed him across the front of his face. My husband had been pastor at this particular church for over 14 years and nothing like this had ever happened. I felt totally out of control. I inwardly screamed, "Why did these boys do this to my son?" Then I prayed, "Oh God, where are You? Why didn't You protect my son? You know how long I have served You, and You know I have given You everything! All I have ever asked for is protection for my family!"

All I could think of was the fact that Scott was going to graduate this year. This was his special year! To think that he would have to walk down the aisle with a huge slash across his face! Would Scott understand? Would he become bitter? We had already been struggling with him through some "teen" pressures and life had not been easy at this crucial age.

The ambulance rushed Scott to the hospital along with his dad. There he received 53 stitches inside and outside on his face. The slash was such that a plastic surgeon was required, along with $1,500 cash. At the time, we were pastoring a small church which could not offer us medical insurance. We now faced the dilemma of finding $1,500.

These were very dark days for me. Tears blurred my vision as I tried to find some answers. I missed my mother, and the grief was very raw. On top of her passing, now I felt as if my family had been violated. I began to pray like my mother had prayed, but still unable to cope, I did not attend school for several days. Instead I made my way to a nearby park with my Bible and begged God for answers. I prayed — or tried to pray — but no answers came. I questioned God over and over again, "Why did You allow this to happen to my son? What are You trying to prove in my life or Scott's life? He is scarred forever; he will never be the same!" I would open the Word of God that I had read every day of my life. Surely the answer

would be there. The first Scripture I turned to and read was, "Vengeance is mine saith the Lord."

"But God I want vengeance! I want to find those boys and see that justice is received!"

fear began to grip my heart, and worse yet, anger. It was like a huge spirit that engulfed me every minute of my life. Where, oh where, would I find relief?

Three days after Scott's accident, my husband was involved in an accident that broke his left arm in three different places and required facial stitches. What was happening to our family? Where was God? Why was He forsaking us?

I suppose Scott's accident, along with my mother's death and my husband's accident was just more than I could bear. I felt myself building a box, and refusing to let anyone inside that box. For weeks, even months, I wandered aimlessly the streets of our city, looking for the boys who had so brutally injured my son for life. Did people try to encourage me? Yes, they did. Did people pray for me? Yes, they did. Did I pray for myself? Yes, I did, but I was hurting very deeply.

It took several months for healing to begin taking place in my heart. Part of the healing came from my precious son, Scott. I had taught him to pray as a child, to forgive and to trust in God. Now he was teaching me. He would come into my bedroom at night, kneel by my bed and say, "Mom, you have to forgive those boys and ask God to save them." He said, "I have forgiven them and I am praying for them."

I felt convicted in my heart, and began asking God to forgive me for my bitterness and anger. How can I be so unforgiving when the offense was not even towards me? The Lord gave me a Scripture in the night: Psalm 37:1-2, "Fret not thyself because of evildoers . . . for they shall soon be cut down like the grass, and wither as the green herb!"

I began to pray and ask the Lord to save the boys who had done this terrible act to my son.

The Lord began to turn the anger into peace. I began to understand the true meaning of "the peace that passes understanding."

Soon I realized my heart was not intent anymore on "finding" the boys so that justice could be served. I placed the boys (five of them whose ages ranged from 8 to 15) in the hands of a merciful God. I knew that the Lord would bring them to justice. Approximately one year after the slashing, a neighboring pastor called our home and said that a young man had prayed at his altar and had confessed that he knew the young men who had slashed our son. He said that the young man was ready to do whatever to make things "right" and would we like to proceed? We had a family meeting with Scott, and together as a family, we wept and agreed that surely God had intervened and we were happy that the Lord had answered our prayer. We closed the case and chose not to pursue legal actions! Thank God for the miracles HE performs!

Victims of Violence, an organization for innocent victims had been working with us from the beginning and had offered financial, medical and counseling assistance. Plastic surgery was an option for Scott. However, Scott chose not to have plastic surgery; therefore, the scar will remain for a lifetime on my son's face. It has been nine years since my son was slashed on the front steps of our church. The doctors informed us that had the slash been a 64th of an inch deeper in Scott's face, he would have never been able to move that side of his face again. That means he would have never smiled again. Today, we have a 25 year old who has a beautiful smile and who uses the scar on his face as a testimony to the wonderful mercy of God!

In the stillness of the night sometimes, I see how God has traced His fingerprints across our lives. Mother is singing with the angels and is better off than ever before. The scar on Jonathan Scott's face is a constant reminder of God's miraculous mercy. My husband's arm healed but most of all God taught us that He never forsakes us. He is always there if we will just pray a prayer of trust and faith. His goodness has penetrated the evil that was forced upon us and He has made all things well. I am so thankful that my mother taught me to pray, that I found my answers through prayer, and that I was able to teach my son how to pray. It is from generation to generation — the gift of prayer and God's mercy!   —Berni Cupoli

Berni Cupoli and son Scott

A Glimpse at the Past

a prayer chain started by mother

When David Talmage, the father of the famous preacher, T. DeWitt Talmage, was an eighteen-year-old boy still living at home with his brother Jacob and his sister, one night the three of them were going to a party.

Their mother, who was an invalid, just before they left, called them to her bedside and said, "You are going out to a party, but I want you to know that I shall be on my knees praying for you until you return."

They went, and on their return passed their mother's door at two o'clock, catching a glimpse of her still kneeling by her bed.

Early the next morning, Mother Talmage wakened her husband and asked him to get up and see what was the matter, for she heard someone weeping. Going hastily down to the living room Father Talmage found his daughter on her knees weeping, but when he undertook to speak to her, she said, "Go to the barn, Father, for David is in worse need of you than I am. I shall be all right."

Going to the barn the old gentleman found David weeping his heart out from the mighty conviction that had seized him. However, when Mr. Talmage had prayed a short time with him, David said, "Go to Jacob; he needs you more than I do now, I presume. He's in the wagon shed."

So it turned out that the Lord saved all three of the Talmage children that morning, in answer to the determined and definite praying of their mother.

David had a sweetheart living down the lane, and rising from his knees, he went right down to her home and told her the wonderful news about himself and his brother and sister being saved, urging her to give her heart to God.

In the prayer there they had together she, too, was added to the host of the redeemed. The news reaching the church produced a tremendous sensation, and a gracious and widespread revival followed!

This sweetheart of David's later became the mother of T. De Witt Talmage. Some years afterward she made a solemn covenant with four other women to meet with them every Wednesday afternoon and pray for their children, until every child in the five homes was saved.

—HERALD OF HIS COMING

the gift of life

the Christmas lights were up, carols were playing constantly on the stereo, and people were bustling about making ready for the Christmas holidays. We were like everyone else — preparing for Christmas.

Little did we know that this Christmas season would begin one of the darkest periods of our life. It was just a normal day when suddenly our world turned upside down. On December 1, 1987, the doctors diagnosed Jonathan, our fifteen-year-old son, with acute lymphocyte leukemia. My mind kept telling me this was a nightmare and I would wake up soon. "Surely this couldn't be happening to our family," I thought. This is something you read about other people facing and thanked God for your healthy children. Reality soon set in and we began a three-year fight to save our son's life.

Jonathan was just three months away from turning sixteen and looking forward to driving and all the freedom that comes from that age. He was working part-time and saving every dime he made. His grandpa, uncle, and dad promised to help him get his car. He was a junior in high school on the honor roll, played the bass guitar for the church youth choir, and loved to play baseball and basketball. At fifteen he was already a six-foot-tall, 170-pound, good-looking guy. More than all that he had a personal relationship with God. As a mother I was so proud of him.

Jonathan had been feeling weak and tired for several months, and developed a pain in his leg, so I took him to the doctor. The doctor at that time focused more on the pain in his leg than he did on his fatigue. He gave him pain medication and told us that if it persisted to bring him back. Jonathan grew weaker but he did not tell us, thinking he was just imagining it. He thought that if something was wrong the doctor would have known. He continued to keep up with all his activities, even though it was a struggle, during this time of weakness.

The story really began on Thanksgiving day. Our family gath-

ered to celebrate the holiday with my side of the family. One of my sisters from out of town had not seen Jonathan for quite some time and commented that he looked thin and pale. When you are with someone day in and day out, you sometimes do not notice a change in their appearance as much. Drawing our attention to his pale countenance, we saw that he did look bad. I asked him how he felt. His reply was that he felt terrible. I decided to take him back to the doctor the next Monday.

I tried not to worry, but it was a difficult thing to do. I was glad when Monday came, so we could get some answers. When we walked into the same doctor's office, he took one look at Jonathan and said, "I can tell he is very anemic. We need to run some blood tests." He told me to make an appointment for three days later and he would have the results from the tests back by then. I received a call from him three hours later telling me I needed to get him to a hematologist that day if possible. He said, "Your son only has about one third of the blood he should have. His hemoglobin count should be 15.0 and Jonathan's count is only 5.11."

I still had no idea what all this meant, but a heavy weight had settled on my heart. I called a hematologist, Dr. Patel, who became a wonderful friend to our family. It was already 4:00 p.m., but they gave me an appointment for the next morning. When we arrived at the doctor's office, he had all of Jonathan's blood work in his hand. He had already called the hospital and made arrangements for them to give Jonathan a transfusion that consisted of three pints of blood. Dr. Patel took us to his office and informed us that our son was very sick. He did not see how he was still walking around. He told us that Jonathan would need a bone marrow aspiration and other tests to determine why he was losing his blood. I asked the doctor what he thought. His reply was, "Let's not borrow trouble. It could be a number of things: aplastic anemia, leukemia, or several other things."

Fear began to grip my heart even more. On Tuesday, we admitted Jonathan to Greater Bakersfield Memorial Hospital to begin these tests but it would be the next day before the results would be available. On Wednesday, December 3, Dr. Patel found my husband and me outside Jonathan's room. He said, "Mr. & Mrs. Mullings, I am so sorry, your son has a very advanced form of leukemia! Ninety-nine percent of his bone marrow cells are blast cells. We might help him live for six months if we're lucky."

I felt my world crashing to my feet. The thought of losing my only son was more than I could bear. When the doctor uttered those words, I collapsed into my husband's arms and we both sobbed uncontrollably together. After our tears had subsided somewhat, we remembered the promise that God would not put more on us than we could bear without making a way of escape.

meanwhile, Jonathan was in his hospital room and knew that we had been waiting for the doctor to come and tell us what the test results were, so we could not put off telling him. After we had cried and

pulled ourselves together as much as possible, we went into his room. He took one look at us and said, "Well, what's up?"

His dad, with still a wet tear on his cheek, walked over to where he lay and sat on the edge of the bed. He took and held one of Jonathan's hands that had lost some of its strength and with trembling lips relayed the dismal message: "Buddy, we've got a big problem." Then he relayed to him what the doctor had just told us. Hot tears began to roll down Jonathan's face. Together, as an orchestra plays musical notes that portray the mournful sound of a tragic dirge, we all three, bound together in grief, sobbed our hearts out for a few minutes.

Suddenly when we felt as if our hearts could not take any more pain, there was a presence that filled the room; it was a peace that only comes from God. That's when Jonathan looked up at his dad and said, "Well, Dad, you've preached faith all my life. Now we're just going to have to live it."

At that moment I did not have a lot of regrets in how I had raised him. I am not saying that I was perfect, but I had done the best I knew how. I was so thankful that I had not waited until a crisis came, to instill a faith and trust in God into our son.

Also for me was a moment of truth. In the time of crisis, I did not have to go to God with my hands behind my back to ask for help and strength. To the best of my ability, I had always tried to put God first in my life. Now, I did not have to become a beggar and bargain with God such as, "If you'll heal my son, I'll live for you, or change my ways." All I knew how to do was to stand on His promises.

We also knew that the only thing that would keep our son alive was prayer made to God for Him to send a miracle. Prayer was not something we only did before we went to bed at night. We chose to make it our lifestyle. We knew the devil could not take Jonathan from us, for we had given him to God.

It was up to God if we got to keep him a little longer. I cannot adequately describe the many emotions I felt the next few hours and days. The old song, "'Tis So Sweet to Trust in Jesus," was my song in the night. When you trust in Jesus, you can know for a fact that no matter what happens, it is going to be all right!

Jonathan told us that he did not think he was going to die, and of course, he did not want to, but either way he was a winner! I cannot think of anything more horrible than to see your child facing death with fear. His peace and faith were such a comfort. The scriptures in the Bible really came alive for us. We quoted 2 Corinthians 5:8: "We are confident, I say, and willing rather, to be absent from the body and to be present with the Lord," and Philippians 1:21: "For me to live in Christ, and to die is gain." We did not want Jonathan to die, but we were facing reality, while hanging on to faith.

dr. Patel wanted to send us to the children's hospital in Los Angeles where he wanted his friend, Dr. Seigel, to see Jonathan. Dr. Stewart Seigel is Head of Oncology at L.A.C.N. He was involved with research cures for cancer and was not taking new patients, but he agreed to see Jonathan. We met with him on December 6 around 10:30 a.m. in the conference room. He explained to us all the medicines, head radiation, spinal taps, and bone marrow aspirations Jonathan would need in the fight to save his life. He also explained to us the chemotherapy drugs he was going to give him that still were in the experimental stage. Because our son's prognosis was diagnosed as very poor, he felt that this was the best that he had to offer. He was very kind, but very blunt! He gave us many things to read and sign, and material that told about the side effects and dangers of the drugs. He said we had to prepare ourselves for the worst. He was realistic in a positive way. I wanted to know about statistics. He told me that none of that mattered. Even if he could tell me that Jonathan had a ninety-nine percent chance of surviving and if he was the one percent that did not survive, it would not matter. It would be a fight, but we knew that we had to try.

It was a three-year emotional roller coaster ride with thirty-seven blood transfusions, numerous spinal taps and injections, bone marrow tests and radiation therapy. There were prayers going up all around the world for him. My main prayer was that God would protect all of Jonathan's vital organs. While the chemotherapy works to kill bad cells, it can also do major damage to the other cells. They told us that head radiation could destroy some brain cells and stunt his growth. It could also damage his teeth and eyes and there was a high probability of sterilization.

The only thing that kept us sane and gave us hope during this horrible ordeal was knowing that God was with us! During this three-year period that seemed as if it would last forever, fear and doubt would overwhelm us, but then we would feel God's peace bear us up, surrounding us like a warm blanket.

how many hot tears did I shed? How many dark days did I live? How can you describe the awfulness of staring death in the face, and it going on and on for such a long time? How can you relate how it feels to walk the hospital hallways day after day, experiencing pain and depression? Unless you live it, you cannot really know how it feels. It is a lonely, self-searching time filled with trouble that just will not disappear. You live it, eat it, and rub shoulders with it. It is there in the morning, throughout the day and when you go to bed at night.

Often even on a spring day, I fought back the veil of tears that blurred the scenery surrounding the hospital grounds. Everything seemed to be exploding with life while I felt cold, alone and crushed, and at times even forsaken.

But I would like to tell you that God was

there also, and friends. If I had not had a private place of prayer to share my feelings with God, and release the overwhelming pressure, the story probably would have ended differently.

We give all praise to God for sustaining Jonathan and giving him back his life! Since Jonathan was already six feet tall, we did not have to worry about

his height. He did grow another one and a half inches. He graduated from West High School, and was the fifteenth top scholar out of a six-hundred-student body. He also graduated Magna Cum Laude with a degree in science from the Cal State University of Bakersfield. In December 1992, he married his high school sweetheart who had stood by him through all his years of sickness, bald head and all. He worked as a geologist for Occidental Oil Company for five years before going full time into the ministry. He has a five-and-half-year-old son, Brett, and he and his wife had a new baby daughter in July 2000!

Aside from giving Jonathan back his life, God kept his brain cells from being destroyed, his growth from being stunted, his eyes from being damaged and he definitely did not become sterile. For ten years he has been cancer free and at his last physical, the doctor declared him in perfect health.

a s a mother of an only son, I am thankful to God that He heard my prayers as well as the prayers of others, that he gave Jonathan back to us, and now He is giving us grandchildren. Every day I am reminded of the miracle of life that God gave to us and will ever be grateful. There is a scripture verse that sprang forth out of the pages of the Bible and came to pass for our family concerning this heart-rending crisis. It is found in Isaiah 63:3, and is filled with promise: "To appoint unto them that mourn . . . to give them beauty for ashes, the oil of joy for mourning, the garment of praise for the spirit of heaviness."

—Laquita Mullings

Laquita Mullings with son Jonathan

saved from the fire

life is not always predictable. Certain things happen when we least expect them to, but often God has ways of warning His children, if they will only listen to His voice. Little did I know that a seemingly insignificant move to another city would hold such significance for us.

In 1995 our family moved to Brockton, Massachusetts to help in a small church that was struggling. My daughter, Danielle, moved to Brockton also, but instead of living with us, she and a friend rented an apartment there together. In 1997 Danielle's friend moved to Virginia, leaving Danielle alone.

On Saturday, February 22, 1997, my daughter and I spent the evening together at the mall. We laughed and chatted about everything, and had such a good time. After we came home from shopping, I tried to get her to spend the night with me. I knew that she had been fearful of staying by herself since her roommate had moved. I asked her several times to spend the night, because some days before, I had a premonition and fear that something bad was going to happen. So I had been praying fervently that God's angels would be around her and keep her safe, but she wanted to be brave and courageous and decided to go on home to her apartment. Her main fear was entering the apartment alone because it was rather dark.

When she got there she called me to let me know that she had made it home OK. As we began to talk, I told her, "Danielle, I've been interceding for God to give His angels charge over you and over your apartment. And I know that you may be fearful, but you don't have to worry about anything. God has given me an assurance that everything is going to be all right." We hung up about midnight. I prayed the Word several times before going to bed: "For he shall give his angels charge over thee, to keep thee in all thy ways. They shall bear thee up in their hands, lest thou dash thy foot against a stone" (Psalm 91:11-12). I said, "Lord, send those angels to Danielle tonight."

Around 3:30 in the morning, I got a call to come to the emergency room at the hospital, because my daughter Danielle had been brought there. My heart began beating very fast. They didn't give me any information and I couldn't imagine what had happened. I thought that if Danielle had gotten sick, she would have called me first, but she had not done that. I wondered if someone had broken into her apartment and I began to imagine all kinds of things, but I knew that God was committed. I knew that He had made some promises and everything would be all right.

When I walked into the emergency room, I learned that there had been a fire in Danielle's apartment building. When I saw her, she was covered with black soot, wearing an oxygen mask and crying. As I comforted her (and rejoiced that she was alive!), others began to tell me the story of what had happened that night. A lady and her teenage daughter lived in the apartment below Danielle. The daughter had put some oil in a pan, put it on the stove, turned the burner on high and then went to bed. They were not sure about the sequence of events after that, but the building caught fire and the alarms went off. There were several people from the fire department who told us that in most cases people do not take fires seriously. The alarms go off from time to time and people get used to hearing them. However, the people in the building finally realized that this time it was serious and everyone in the building got out except Danielle. Her apartment was on the third floor, and she was so quiet that the others forgot about her.

When Danielle heard the alarms she decided to go to her front door and tell someone else about the alarm. When she opened the door, fire knocked her backwards and chased her into her bedroom. She opened her window and tore off the screen. When she looked outside and saw all the people from her apartment building, she said, "Please, help me down."

There was a policeman on the scene, but it was his job to keep her inside until the fire department got there. However, when the fire department arrived, there was a wall around her building that prevented the fire trucks from having access to where she was.

As Danielle stood looking out the window, the smoke billowed out from around her head. She had a white T-shirt on, and she put her nose underneath the shirt to try to keep from breathing the smoke. But when she did, the smoke engulfed the shirt. When I saw the shirt at the hospital it was completely black on the outside and on the inside. Danielle thought she was going to die. She began to scream frantically, "Please, don't let me die here! I don't want to die like this!" But the policeman would not let her come down.

a man who lived in the apartment was a body builder. He told us that when he walked around the building, he saw the smoke rolling out around her head like a towering inferno. When he looked toward the window, he could not see her face anymore, but he could hear her saying, "I feel the fire." He remembered his own daughter and yelled up to her, "Jump, baby, jump!" And she did. She fell three floors, barely scraping the building with her leg, and the man caught her.

The story was reported on CNN and also made the front page of the *Boston Globe* and several other major newspapers in the Boston area. The papers called it "A Leap of Faith." I couldn't think of anything better to call it myself.

Danielle only weighs 115 pounds, but they told us that the pressure of her weight falling that far could have literally killed the man that caught her. I am so glad he was there! And I will forever be grateful to him. I really feel that he was almost like an angel of God.

When we went back to the apartment to survey the damage, everything was totally destroyed except one plaque on the wall by the window from where Danielle jumped. I walked over to it and wiped the black soot off and there was a picture of an angel watching over a young girl, with the words, "He will give His angels charge over thee."

What if I, her mother, had not prayed so fervently when I felt the premonition? What if I had not prayed the Word over her until I felt peace? God saved my daughter from the fire. She was not burned. She had no broken bones. She was not asphyxiated from the smoke. She jumped from a third story window — safe and sound. Nothing was wrong with her except a mild foot injury from scraping the side of the building. I know God sent an angel to keep her and carry her down to safety. It was a miracle!

—Sheila Clark

Sheila Clark with daughter Danielle

A Glimpse at the Past

one glimpse of her in prayer

Once I suddenly opened the door of mother's room, and saw her on her knees beside her chair, and heard her speak my name in prayer. I quickly and quietly withdrew, with a feeling of awe and reverence in my heart. Soon I went away from home to school, then to college, then into life's sterner duties.

But I never forgot that one glimpse of my mother at prayer, nor the one word — my name — which I heard her utter. Well did I know what I had seen that day was but a glimpse of what was going on every day in that sacred closet of prayer and the consciousness strengthened me a thousand times in duty, in danger, and in struggle. And when death came at length and sealed those lips, the sorest sense of loss that I felt was the knowledge that no more would my mother be praying for me.

—J.R. MILLER

the command

from birth, both of my daughters (Victoria in particular) had suffered from chronic eczema. Their condition was so severe that their bodies were covered with scabs from their scalps to their ankles.

Although this condition is not life threatening, it is extremely painful and disfiguring. Many mornings they would awaken with blood caked under their fingernails from scratching their rashes during the night. They were allowed to bathe only every other day and were permitted to use soap only once every four days. They were not allowed many of the activities of normal children, including swimming in chlorinated water, or even playing in the sprinklers in the sunshine.

This condition also exacted an emotional toll on them. Often I would find Victoria looking in the mirror at her face. She would cry and say, "Why isn't my skin pretty like my friends? Why am I so ugly?" As a parent, it was heart-rending to be unable to answer her questions. We always answered, "You are only as pretty as you are on the inside." However, from a child's standpoint, this answer was inadequate.

From their births, we had seen many doctors and specialists. We tried every treatment and medication available to children their ages. This included intense steroid treatments and hydrocortisone cream. One doctor even recommended that we rub them with Crisco shortening every night before putting them to bed. We tried all these treatments to no avail.

Finally at our last doctor's appointment, Victoria's doctor told me, "Mrs. Ezell, this is a chronic condition. She will never be rid of this. All we can do is teach her to take care of it." I left with a very heavy heart and a very disappointed daughter.

Many times I petitioned God through prayer and even fasting to heal my daughters, and even joined with other women in prayer for their healing. I exhausted every avenue known to me.

In June 1995 I attended a ladies' retreat that took us away from everyday life. We were tucked away from everything, breathing fresh mountain air. Not only were we breathing fresh air in the natural, but at the service that night, the speaker led us into a depth of the spirit that I had never before experienced. As we prayed, the speaker stopped us and said that there were special circumstances in the service. He told us that there was an open door between heaven and earth

and anything we commanded would be done. He quoted the scripture, "If ye shall ask anything in my name, I will do it" (John 14:14). At this place in prayer, it seemed that God said to me, "Ask Me to heal your daughters." So I did. Then, according to what the minister told us to do, and with tears running like a river down my cheeks, I commanded the eczema to leave my daughters. It was such a release for me, and I felt such a surge of power.

When I returned home the next day that command was far from my mind. We were in a hurry to attend a birthday party and I rushed the girls into the bathtub.

Then I went to clean the kitchen. As I was washing the dishes, Victoria came running into the kitchen. "Mama, Mama," she cried, "my eczema is gone!" I looked at her arms, her legs, and her face and every scab was gone! They had washed off in the tub.

It has been several years and there has been no recurrence of eczema on either of the girls. I even gave away their special creams, lotions and soaps.

This dramatic healing of my daughters reminds me of the following scripture, "And as Jesus passed by, he saw a man which was blind from his birth. And his disciples asked him, saying, Master, who did sin, this man or his parents, that he was born blind? Jesus answered, neither hath this man sinned, nor his parents; but that the works of God be made manifest in him" (John 9:1-3).

I will always be grateful that God heard my cry and healed our whole family. The emotional trauma of this condition was taking a toll on all of us. Now when I look at their clear skin, a tingle of delight and thanksgiving pulsates through my very being. I know that God still answers prayers, because He did it for me!

BETH EZELL

A Glimpse at the Past
a mother's kiss and her prayers

Dr. Joseph Parker once said that when Robert Moffat was added to the Kingdom of God, a whole continent was added with him. A mother's kiss did it. He was leaving home, and his mother was going with him part of the way.

At last she could walk no farther, and she stopped. "Robert," she said, "promise me something."

"What?" asked the boy.

"Promise me something," she said again, and he replied, "You will have to tell me before I will promise."

"It is something you can easily do," she said. "Promise your mother."

He looked into her face, and said, "Very well, Mother, I will do anything you wish."

She clasped her hands behind his head and pulled his face down to hers, and said, "Robert, you are going out into a wicked world. Begin every day with God. Close every day with God."

Then she kissed him. Every day of the year, Robert Moffat's mother prayed for her boy until he became the missionary that he was.

—METHODIST RECORDER

63

broken dreams

august 1, 1998 it was finally going to happen. I was so excited. The reception hall was reserved, the caterers had a final menu, candelabras were on hold, payments had been made to the photographer, and the videographer had been chosen. Songs were ready, ministers prepared and our families notified. We had purchased over 20,000 lights; after all, this was going to be quite the affair. Aisle bouquets were being finished, dresses and tuxedos were being chosen. It was everything a young girl dreams about.

In the past I had wondered if my dream would ever come true, or if my knight in shining armor would ever ride in on his white horse. Would it ever be my turn? But then, it happened! Wedding catalogs and invitation samples were strung around my apartment, while rolls of ribbon and bunches of flowers lined the closets. There were so many decisions to make, so many choices available, but oh, each and every decision was exciting to make.

I had met John* September 15, 1996 at Chili's restaurant. Several of my friends were eating there, so I went to join them. I inadvertently ended up at a table with my cousin. Along with her, there were two nice young men sitting there. We talked and laughed and had a great time. My 23rd birthday was the next day, and I was complaining of how old I was getting, until it became a big joke and we laughed about it.

I couldn't help but notice that one of the guys was very handsome. I had seen him at church before, but had no idea who he was. There were so many college students that attended our church I was never able to keep track of them all. A couple of weeks later, we had a youth barbecue at my parents' home. We invited several college kids, including the two young men that I had met at Chili's. One showed up, but unfortunately it was not John. Apparently, he had become too nervous to come. I was so disappointed. I had planned for him to be there, hoping that we could get to know each other a little better.

That night, one of my friends called him and then handed the phone to me. We hit it off, and that first phone call lasted until 2:00 a.m. Many phone calls followed, and it wasn't long until we were an official couple.

John was wonderful. He was so meek and sweet; everyone loved him. He had come to attend the Christian college in our town, and since he was from another country he was not allowed to work in the United States while he was a student here. Because of his inability to hold a regular job, he wasn't able to spend money on me the way a young man normally does, but he made up for it in many other ways. He treated me wonderfully, and was constantly building me up and telling me how beautiful I was. He had one of the most tender, kind hearts that I had ever seen in a person.

John was also very talented. As a theology

student, he was very knowledgeable of the Bible, and a great speaker. He had a way of making the audience feel at ease. He was also incredible with music. He could play several instruments and had the most beautiful voice. He sang in a group which made an album, and because of this they were asked to sing at many different events.

John was also a very hard worker and people began to take notice. He was always doing more than was expected in school. The students and staff fell in love with him and voted him as their student body president. He seemed to be perfect, and I was the lucky girlfriend.

About five months after meeting John, a door of opportunity opened for me and my best girl friend to go and help out in a new church being established on the East Coast. It would only be for one year, and my parents thought it would be a good test for John and me.

Three months later, my best friend, Nicole* and I said our tearful good-byes to family and friends and were on our way. It was the first time either of us had officially moved away from home, so it was bittersweet. Then the excitement hit! These two West Coast girls were moving clear across the country. The 3,000-mile drive was long and we could hardly wait to get there.

When we arrived, we quickly found an apartment and jobs, then settled into our new life. It was everything we dreamed of: we sang, taught Sunday school,

planned church banquets, counseled and started a young girls' group. We worked full-time jobs and then worked for the church. We loved every minute of it. Life was grand! I had the most wonderful family praying for me and supporting me, and my sweet John was home waiting for me, and training for his work in the ministry. I dreamed of the day when we could work in a church together.

John and I made the long distance relationship work. Of course, we also kept AT&T in business! John was great about sending the sweetest, longest love letters to me. They were filled with his dreams for us and he was always encouraging me, making me laugh. I couldn't wait for the day that the miles would no longer separate us.

That Christmas, I flew to John's home with him to meet his family. I had a wonderful time with them and we got along perfectly. By this time, John and I had fully discussed marriage. This is the reason that I had flown home with him to meet his family.

One month later I flew home to California to attend a conference there. Wednesday morning, John and my parents picked me up from the airport. Thursday afternoon, John took me to a little practice piano room at the college and played and sang a song he had written for me. I cried as he sang the beautiful words of love. That Friday night, John took me to the waterfront and proposed. He pulled out a beautiful diamond ring. It had one solitaire in the middle, with three rows of baguettes on each side of the band. I loved it and was so proud to wear it. I finally belonged to someone and I had a ring of proof on my left hand. We decided that August 1, 1998 would be the perfect day.

I returned to the East Coast with thoughts of a wedding dancing in my head. Planning a West Coast wedding from the East Coast was no easy task and was very stressful, but we did it. Everything in my life seemed so perfect. Every pain, every problem, every trial, every tear all seemed to fade away with the promise of this marriage. I had stars in my eyes and everyone around me had halos on their heads. It was such a dream. Then suddenly, in an instant, without any warning, my beautiful dream turned into my darkest nightmare.

I can remember exactly where I was sitting when I heard the news. Actually, it was an accident that I found out. It was just a coincidence that I made that phone call — then again, maybe it wasn't.

anticipating my upcoming wedding and move back to the West Coast in May, I had begun to search for another position within the company for which I was working.finally found one, so on Friday afternoon, February 13, 1998, on the spur of the moment, I decided to telephone my dad's office to tell him that I had located a job in California. I had to tell someone!

His secretary informed me that he had just left the office with a man named John. "John, why that's my fiancé," I responded. Then I thought, *What could my dad possibly be doing in the middle of the day with my fiancé?* Then it hit me. The next day was Valentine's Day. Of course! They were planning something special for me.

I quickly called my mother at home, expecting to catch her involved as well. "Where's Dad?" I asked. "At the office," she responded.

"He is not," I shot back, "he's with John. I just

called there and his secretary told me they were out together."

Then I asked, "What are they up to?" Dead silence. "Hello, Mom, hello?"

"Jennifer, you need to pray." This is all she would say. She repeated it over and over that I needed to pray. I started to panic. Someone must have been in a car accident. I begged and pleaded with her to tell me but she didn't want to. After much convincing, she said that there had been some accusations brought against John at the college, and that my dad was meeting with him to discuss the issues.

"Accusations? What kind of accusations?" I asked in shocked disbelief.

"There have been accusations brought forth from a woman, and she is claiming many terrible things have happened between her and John."

At first I thought it was a joke, but then finally I realized that it was very real and ugly. My body turned ice cold. It was as if I had turned into a robot. I remember walking to my supervisor's office, stating that I had an emergency and walking out the door. Thank

God it was Friday and I would have at least a weekend to grasp the severity of the situation. I really don't remember driving home. I just remember that somehow, I made it through the heavy, Washington, D.C. traffic without even noticing anything or anyone around me. Nothing registered for I was in pure shock.

When I arrived at my apartment, I just sat down on the couch, feeling like a three-hundred-pound weight had been attached to my body. My arms and legs were immovable. Moving a finger seemed like a huge task. I stared into space. Surely I will wake up soon and find this to be a nightmare. Surely this cannot be happening to me, I thought.

My parents called the pastor of the church where I was helping out, as well as my roommate. The pastor and his wife, and my roommate all rushed to the apartment and I began to sob uncontrollably. They all tried to comfort and console me, but we were all shocked at what was happening.

That night John finally called me. I had been waiting. I wanted so much to hear him say that it wasn't true, that it was all lies, but in the back of my mind, I knew it wouldn't happen. He simply said, "It's true, Jen. It's true."

There was so much more to the story than I had even begun to imagine. Apparently he had been involved in pornography. Numerous sites on the Internet had been accessed over several months. He had also made several phone calls to pornographic lines. He had relationships with several other women during the time we were together. Even up to the night before I arrived in California to become engaged, he had shared a room with another woman. Fornication and vile acts were performed. At the same time he was professing his faith to me, encouraging me in my ministry, he was professing his profound love for me and also the president of the student body. It was more than I could take. To say that I was devastated would be a gross understatement. I cannot find the words to describe the despair that I felt. I only can describe my reactions.

I could not leave my apartment until the following week. I rolled on the floor, screaming and crying in agony. How could this happen? How could God have let this happen? How could someone not have known this was going on? I spoke to this man literally every single day on the phone, and yet I had not one clue that anything was happening. He spent time with my parents and family. He spent time with teachers and pastors. How did he hide this hideous problem from so many people? The questions raced back and forth through my mind. I could not sleep for days. I would lay in my bed and cry until 2:00 or 3:00 in the morning while my friend, Nicole, sat on the side of the bed. Finally, in pure exhaustion, I would fall asleep, only to awaken screaming about 5:00 in the morning. Immediately I would call my parents, not even saying hello when they answered the phone, and just cry and cry. There was no peace. Eating was out of the question. The thought of food made me gag. After almost two weeks of almost no food, the people at work became so concerned that they went out and bought a little hamburger from McDonald's for me one day. I was only able to take about two or three bites.

I was once so particular about my dress.

Now Nicole tried to comb my hair for me in the mornings because it seemed impossible for me to handle. Every bit of hope seemed gone. All the lights had gone out. I felt like I had nothing to live for. I could not even pray for myself. I only cried and asked God, "Why?"

I began to beg God to let me die. I had no desire to live. Nothing mattered to me. I was angry with people, with John, with the women involved and with God. The sight of anyone happy made me furious. That is what I used to be — happy. It wasn't fair. It was also a very public affair. My friends and family everywhere knew the ugly details of the situation. There was no escape. I was humiliated and ready to give up.

On the advice of my pastor, I returned home to California in March. The women who had been involved with John were still attending my church. I was in agony. Some of

them had no remorse. It was just the lifestyle they lived. My family, on the other hand, was deeply damaged. I stayed in my room for almost three months. I could not walk through the mall. Anything and everything set me off and I would break into sobs. I was afraid to go any-

where because I no longer had control of my own emotions.

Now I will tell the most important part of the story. I survived! When I did not have the strength to pray for myself, my family and friends spent hours on their knees praying for me. Their prayers are responsible for my life. I sincerely believe that I would not be alive today if it were not for prayer.

This trial has deepened my walk with God. I learned to trust Him and depend on Him when it seemed like there was no other hope in my life. I learned that although the sun may not always shine, it is only in the darkest night you can see the brilliance of the stars!

Although many people prayed for me, I want to give special recognition to my mother. She never gave up praying until God healed my mind completely. Her loving concern carried me through my "valley of death." It was her prayers that brought healing to my emotions and made me want to live again.

The sun is shining again. There is laughter; there is the singing of the birds, and there is hope! Life is good, all because of the faithfulness of a God who answers His children's prayers. "For the eyes of the Lord are over the righteous, and his ears are open unto their prayers" (1 Peter 3:12).

God took my broken dreams and mended them, building into my life a deeper compassion for others. In many ways, my brokenness became a stepping stone to greater things in God. I found out that no experience is wasted when God gets involved with it. I am thankful that my mother persevered and made sure that God kept His finger on this broken vessel, and made it over anew!

—JENNIFER LARSON

*Names have been changed to protect identities.

kept by two women

Would you believe me if I told you I had two mothers praying for me all my life, and I did not even know about one of them until I was about 19 years old? The prayers of these two mothers kept me even in the midst of temptation and peer pressure while serving in the navy. My parents came to the Lord when I was four years old. When I was seven, my dad felt a call on his life to the ministry, so he attended The Bible Institute in Minnesota. It was a great life surrounded by friends and family. After attending college, my father went to assist at a church in Florida. While living there I received God's Spirit at eleven years of age.

My dad felt God drawing him back to his hometown, so when I was about twelve years old our family headed to Kenosha, Wisconsin. My parents became very active in church and involved in many areas of ministry. While I was in the 7th grade, my parents transferred me from a public school to a Christian school. Then from 8th grade until graduation they home schooled me. I turned seventeen in November and graduated in January.

at this point in my life, I was confronted with many conflicting thoughts and ideas. I thought there might be a calling on my life, but was so confused as to whether the call was from God or my folks. I was really torn and began to question everything. I was not even sure about my own salvation. I ran from the questions and confusion by joining the navy and left home just a few months after my 17th birthday. It is clearly not impossible to live for God while serving in the United States armed forces, but it is certainly not the most pious place to live. As I felt the first breath of freedom from my family and my home church, I found that, for me, it was a time of searching.

I faced the temptations that most young people face. The temptation to drink alcohol was strong. The men on my ship determined to get me drunk and vowed that they would make sure that I would fall into sexual sin, as well. For some reason, my virginity was a real problem for them and they felt challenged to see to it that I lost my innocence.

Looking back, I remember the many nights

when the other guys and I would set off for an evening of fun. It seemed that they were always encouraging me to drink more than I could handle. Then they would introduce me to girls who were looking for just a good time and a temporary fling. Life went on like that for sometime, but in the midst of it all there was something that held me back. Something strong kept pulling me away from the things that were a temptation for me. Something was giving me the strength to stand. Something was pulling me toward God. It was not long before I would discover that the "something" was a prayer-answering God.

My mother prayed for me daily. There were some days she prayed for me continually throughout the day when she felt I was under heavy attack from the enemy. Things I would say to her let her know that confusion filled my mind about my beliefs. It was constant prayer on her part. She based her prayers on God's Word. She believed that His Word was true, and she had faith that God would keep me from sin and bring me back to a deep and personal walk with Him.

Mom's prayers were personal and powerful, and she prayed with authority! She made up her mind that her son was going to serve God and she refused to give in to the pressure of the age.

One night, while stationed in Norfolk, Virginia, I made my way to a church in the city. It was a warm and friendly church and I felt God's presence there. I liked the clean feeling I felt when I was there. Something came over me and I began to pray and repent. When I made peace with God, my mind became clear. The confusion left and I found what I looked for in Him.

eventually, I learned that my future wife Michelle's mother prayed over her four daughters every night. That did not sound too unusual, until I learned that she had been praying for me for many, many years. Her prayers each night was not only for her girls, but from the time they were babies, she prayed for their future spouses. Every day she would talk to God about the young men that her daughters would one day marry. She asked Him to keep His hand on each of their future husbands.

She personally prayed that He would place a shield of protection around me to keep me on the path of righteousness. She asked Him to give me strength to remain pure and holy, and asked Him to prepare me to be the spiritual head of our household. She also prayed that my desire would be to live for God with all of my heart, soul, mind, and strength, and that together my wife and I would be used of God.

Now I understood! Both mothers were praying for me at the same time! "When two or more agree. . . ." Because of their prayers, God kept His hand on my life when I was questioning everything and confused. He kept me pure and holy. He kept me from doing the things that I knew were sin. My shipmates did not succeed in their endeavor to get me drunk and cause me to fall into sexual sin. In fact, I was still on the U.S.S. Yorktown, when Michelle and I married. I believe that some of those men were a bit jealous about the fact that we were both entering our marriage as virgins.

Today, I serve as an assistant pastor. Michelle is the music director. Our church has a Christian academy and my wife and I both work there full time. I teach middle school and serve as the assistant principal and athletic director. Michelle teaches high school. We have three precious children.

God has truly blessed me. He has kept His hand upon me and given me two gifts — a beautiful family and a wonderful church. Where would I be without the two women who had prayed all their lives for me: my mother's prayers, and the prayers of a woman that I did not even know? I will never doubt the power of a mother's prayer. Their prayers kept me! — JAMES KASTEN

when God took over

the disease couldn't have come at a worse time. The Reverend Jack Yonts, my son, and his wife, Lori, had just brought their adopted infant daughter, Lily, home on Valentine's Day 1999.

Five weeks later on March 19, 1999 Jack thought he was coming down with a cold, and went to bed early. At two a.m., he awoke and found he couldn't breathe. Still fighting for breath the next morning, Dan Sharp, his assistant pastor, took Jack to St. Elizabeth Hospital where he was diagnosed with pneumonia and bronchitis. They sent him home with antibiotics.

Bed rest didn't help and by the following Tuesday his condition had deteriorated. He was admitted to Theda Clark Medical Center in Neenah, Wisconsin.

"I really felt like I was going to die that night. I just couldn't get any air," Jack said. During the night, he was moved to the intensive care unit. He was prepped for a lung biopsy to determine the cause of the pneumonia and was put on a ventilator. They took a large part of his lung and sent it to Mayo Clinic, but they could not find what exactly was wrong, so they gave him everything. Lori, his wife, said, "I thought they'd find out what was causing the pneumonia, get him on the right drugs and we'd be home in a day or two." The biopsy was inconclusive.

Lori realized how serious it was becoming and called us. Of course, my husband and I purchased airline tickets and flew from Chicago to Wisconsin to be with our son. By this time, Jack had developed adult respiratory distress syndrome, a condition in which the lungs become inflamed and hardened, leaving them unable to expand on their own.

When we walked into the hospital room we couldn't believe what we saw. Jack's oxygen levels were so low that he was purple from the waist up. Because he unknowingly fought the ventilator, they put him in a self-induced coma. That's when the nightmare began.

It was a three-and-a-half-month vigil by his bedside. For seventeen days, my husband never left the hospital (I stayed in a little home they provided right behind the hospital). It was on Good Friday that the doctors told us to tell Jack goodbye, that he only had two hours to live, but we refused to do so. Instead we went somewhere and prayed. I fervently prayed, "God, I know You are sovereign, but I cannot take the sorrow of losing another child." (Our 26-year-old daughter had been killed in a car accident in 1981.) "You've got to heal Jack!" I began sobbing until I had cried all the tears I could cry. The old sorrow of our daughter's passing surfaced and I felt like my heart was going to break. "God, You've got to do something. I cannot take this pain again. Our son is so young. He is doing such a fine job as pastor. His wife needs him. His new five-week-old baby needs him. We all need him. Don't let him die!"

That same day, Dan Sharp, Jack's assistant pastor, went straight to the church where the special Good Friday service had already begun. He went to the podium, informed the church of their pastor's condition, canceled the regular service, and called a prayer meeting. Sharp recalls, "We prayed for a long time, and eventually the heavy prayers turned to worship."

During this whole ordeal, complete strangers would come into the hospital chapel and pray with us. People would drop by the hospital and pray, cards came saying that churches were praying, phone calls came in daily saying, "We're praying for a miracle."

Over the next eight weeks, 14 holes were blown in his lungs by the ventilator. The treatment was now turning against him. While the machine was forcing oxygen into the hardened tissue of his lungs, the pressure would puncture the lungs, causing them to collapse. Chest tubes were inserted to re-inflate the lungs each time. He began to go into organ failure, with his kidneys, liver, and heart losing ground. "Compounding the 70-percent death rate in ARDS patients is the fact that the percentages increase ten percent with each organ that fails," said Dr. Michael Maguire of Fox Valley Pulmonary Medicine. "Jack had multi-system organ failure, involving the lungs, kidneys, liver, and heart, and he had blood clots in his lungs. We had nothing more to offer him."

Stunning the doctors, Jack once again showed signs of stabilizing as he had done mid-way through the ordeal, and became aware of his surroundings. At this point a team of physicians said a lung transplant was the only option. We were told that Jack would need to be flown to the university hospital in Madison. We were also told that if Jack's body accepted the transplanted lungs, he would still

require medications costing $1,000 to $1,200 a month. He could not drink tap water. He would also not be allowed to go out into crowds, meaning no church services. His life expectancy after a transplant was five to six years. It was a very negative report. That horrible day, standing in that hospital room, seeing the suffering of my son, listening to the jargon of the professionals, everything just seemed suffocating and hopeless. I looked around at the hospital room where we were standing. Every kind of machine imaginable seemed to be in the room. A doctor from the transplant center was sitting by Jack's bed talking into his ear saying, "You're going to die. You're going to have a heart attack." In other words, she was telling him, "You're going to die and everything bad is going to occur if you don't have the lung transplant."

I don't know exactly what happened to me, but something welled up inside of me, and I told my husband, "Go get the head doctor, Dr. Harvey. I want to talk to him." When the doctor walked into the room, I said, "Dr. Harvey, they have my son so traumatized; this is not the way it's going to be. Get them out of here!" As I began to speak, I felt great faith well up inside of me and said, "We have got faith in God that He is going to raise Jack up. We're not going to have the transplant and we don't want to hear anymore about it!" Boldness came over me and I scooted around the room trying to get everyone out of there except the family. As some of the doctors and nurses were leaving the room upon my insistence, they looked at us like we were nuts, but I didn't care. At that moment I was remembering what had transpired several weeks earlier when my son had come out of the self-induced coma. He had struggled to form words about something he had experienced; he could not speak then, but we were able to read his lips. One night he felt somebody was in the room. Then he felt a hand move down and touch his chest. He then knew who that Somebody was. The Lord said to him, "Jack, it's gonna be alright."

When I looked at all those intimidating machines, heard the negative voices around me, and felt the pressure of the medical system, something happened to me. As a mother, I just cleared the room and simply put the case into the hands of God. We had done all we could; it was time for God to take over.

It was on that very day that Jack's condition turned around. He had not been able to sit up or eat, but within five days he was out of the intensive care unit.

Still in bed, he began lifting weights. After two weeks, he was allowed to dangle his legs over the edge of the bed. But Jack was determined to get up. He motioned for them to let him get out of bed and walk. They allowed him to go to the door and back, but only as far as the ventilator tubing would stretch. On June 21, his tracheotomy, which held the ventilator tube, was removed. "I got to speak for the first time," Jack said. "My first words were an enthusiastic, 'Thank you, Jesus!'"

Dr. Michael Maguire of Fox Valley Pulmonary Medicine said these words: "Jack Yonts is no doubt a miracle. He would have had better odds at winning the lottery. I can count maybe three or four miracles during my years of practice, but this definitely tops the list. When we had nothing more to offer him, their prayers took over."

Jack is now back home with his wife, Lori, and their baby celebrating life. He has built a 350-seat new church and is busy working as pastor in the Lord's service. He still enjoys telling people about the day things changed for him. He says, "I remember my mom shaking her finger at the head of the transplant team, and she told them God was going to heal me, and we didn't want to hear anything more about the transplant. She then kicked them all out of my room. They all looked at us like we were nuts."

Yes, I probably did appear to be a little nuts, but I just followed my heart and God sent goodness and mercy to follow us. As a mother, I will always be grateful for the gift of life that was mercifully given to us amid such odds. God is faithful to the prayers of his children and especially to this mother. I will never forget the day that God said, "OK, it's My turn." When He took over, everything changed for the better.

— JOANN YONTS

only God can move mountains, but the prayer of a mother moves the heart of God